Adult
MAD LIBS™

The world's greatest _shower_ game

Baby on Board Mad Libs

by Molly Reisner

PSS!

PRICE STERN SLOAN
An Imprint of Penguin Group (USA) Inc.

PRICE STERN SLOAN
Published by the Penguin Group
Penguin Group (USA) Inc., 375 Hudson Street, New York, New York 10014, USA
Penguin Group (Canada), 90 Eglinton Avenue East, Suite 700, Toronto, Ontario M4P 2Y3, Canada
(a division of Pearson Penguin Canada Inc.)
Penguin Books Ltd, 80 Strand, London WC2R 0RL, England
Penguin Ireland, 25 St Stephen's Green, Dublin 2, Ireland
(a division of Penguin Books Ltd)
Penguin Group (Australia), 707 Collins Street, Melbourne, Victoria 3008, Australia
(a division of Pearson Australia Group Pty Ltd)
Penguin Books India Pvt Ltd, 11 Community Centre, Panchsheel Park, New Delhi—110 017, India
Penguin Group (NZ), 67 Apollo Drive, Rosedale, Auckland 0632, New Zealand
(a division of Pearson New Zealand Ltd)
Penguin Books, Rosebank Office Park, 181 Jan Smuts Avenue, Parktown North 2193, South Africa
Penguin China, B7 Jaiming Center, 27 East Third Ring Road North, Chaoyang District, Beijing 100020, China

Penguin Books Ltd, Registered Offices: 80 Strand, London WC2R 0RL, England

Cover photograph and illustration © Thinkstock

Published by Price Stern Sloan,
a division of Penguin Young Readers Group,
345 Hudson Street, New York, New York 10014.

ISBN 978-0-8431-7290-4
1 3 5 7 9 10 8 6 4 2

ALWAYS LEARNING   PEARSON

Adult MAD LIBS™

INSTRUCTIONS

The world's greatest _shower_ game

MAD LIBS® is a game for people who don't like games!
It can be played by one, two, three, four, or forty.

• RIDICULOUSLY SIMPLE DIRECTIONS

In this book, you'll find stories containing blank spaces where words are left out. One player, the READER, selects one of the stories. The READER shouldn't tell anyone what the story is about. Instead, the READER should ask the other players, the WRITERS, to give words to fill in the blank spaces in the story.

• TO PLAY

The READER asks each WRITER in turn to call out words—adjectives or nouns or whatever the spaces call for—and uses them to fill in the blank spaces in the story. The result is your very own MAD LIBS! Then, when the READER reads the completed MAD LIBS to the other players, they will discover they have written a story that is fantastic, screamingly funny, shocking, silly, crazy, or just plain dumb—depending on the words each WRITER called out.

• EXAMPLE (*Before* and *After*)

" _____ !" he said _____
      EXCLAMATION   ADVERB

as he jumped into his convertible _____ and
                                                NOUN

drove off with his _____ wife.
                              ADJECTIVE

" _____*Ouch*_____ !" he said _____*stupidly*_____
      EXCLAMATION   ADVERB

as he jumped into his convertible _____*cat*_____ and
                                                NOUN

drove off with his _____*brave*_____ wife.
                              ADJECTIVE

In case you have forgotten what adjectives, adverbs, nouns, and verbs are, here is a quick review:

An **ADJECTIVE** describes something or somebody. _Lumpy, soft, ugly, messy,_ and _short_ are adjectives.

An **ADVERB** tells how something is done. It modifies a verb and usually ends in "ly." _Modestly, stupidly, greedily,_ and _carefully_ are adverbs.

A **NOUN** is the name of a person, place, or thing. _Sidewalk, umbrella, bridle, bathtub,_ and _nose_ are nouns.

A **VERB** is an action word. _Run, pitch, jump,_ and _swim_ are verbs. Put the verbs in past tense if the directions say **PAST TENSE**. _Ran, pitched, jumped,_ and _swam_ are verbs in the past tense.

When we ask for **A PLACE**, we mean any sort of place: a country or city (_Spain, Cleveland_) or a room (_bathroom, kitchen_).

An **EXCLAMATION** or **SILLY WORD** is any sort of funny sound, gasp, grunt, or outcry, like _Wow!, Ouch!, Whomp!, Ick!,_ and _Gadzooks!_

When we ask for specific words, like a **NUMBER**, a **COLOR**, an **ANIMAL**, or a **PART OF THE BODY**, we mean a word that is one of those things, like _seven, blue, horse,_ or _head._

When we ask for a **PLURAL**, it means more than one. For example, _cat_ pluralized is _cats._

MAD LIBS® is fun to play with friends, but you can also play it by yourself! To begin with, DO NOT look at the story on the page below. Fill in the blanks on this page with the words called for. Then, using the words you have selected, fill in the blank spaces in the story. Now you've created your own hilarious MAD LIBS® game!

VERB ENDING IN "ING" _____

VERB _____

ADJECTIVE _____

ADJECTIVE _____

PART OF THE BODY _____

VERB _____

NOUN _____

NOUN _____

NOUN _____

PLURAL NOUN _____

NOUN _____

VERB _____

ADJECTIVE _____

PLURAL NOUN _____

ADJECTIVE _____

NOUN _____

NOUN _____

NOUN _____

It's never too early to start _____ about your baby boy's

VERB ENDING IN "ING"

name! To _____ the picking process, here are some ideas

VERB

for _____ monikers and their definitions. Straight

ADJECTIVE

from the _____ Testament, Benjamin means "son of the

ADJECTIVE

right _____." Another oldie is Joseph, meaning "he

PART OF THE BODY

shall _____." A classic choice, Jackson means "God's

VERB

_____." Inspired by a celebrity like Kourtney Kardashian?

NOUN

Try Mason—it literally means " _____ -worker." Looking for

NOUN

sophistication? Sebastian, meaning "revered _____," might suit

NOUN

your _____. Or how about Henry—" _____ ruler"?

PLURAL NOUN _NOUN_

Some more rugged options are the names Hunter, which obviously

means "to _____," and Wyatt, which means " _____

VERB _ADJECTIVE_

warrior." If you're feeling nostalgic for the '90s TV show _Beverly_

_____, _90210_, why not Brandon, meaning " _____

PLURAL NOUN _ADJECTIVE_

hill"? Or the ultimate bad boy name, Dylan, which simply means

" _____ "! Find a name up your _____ ? Now you

NOUN _NOUN_

just need to convince your darling _____ that he loves it, too!

NOUN

Adult MAD LIBS

GIRL NAMES

The world's greatest _shower_ game

MAD LIBS® is fun to play with friends, but you can also play it by yourself! To begin with, DO NOT look at the story on the page below. Fill in the blanks on this page with the words called for. Then, using the words you have selected, fill in the blank spaces in the story. Now you've created your own hilarious MAD LIBS® game!

ADJECTIVE _____

LETTER OF THE ALPHABET_____

VERB ENDING IN "ING" _____

PLURAL NOUN_____

ADJECTIVE _____

ADJECTIVE _____

ADJECTIVE _____

NOUN _____

ADJECTIVE _____

NOUN _____

PLURAL NOUN_____

ADJECTIVE _____

VERB ENDING IN "ING" _____

ADJECTIVE _____

NOUN _____

NOUN _____

NOUN _____

NOUN _____

Adult MAD LIBS™
GIRL NAMES
The world's greatest _shower_ game

Are you having a/an _____ girl and have no idea what
ADJECTIVE

to name her? Check out this _____-list of notable
LETTER OF THE ALPHABET

names and their definitions to get your brain _____!
VERB ENDING IN "ING"

Classic movie _____ are always a/an _____
PLURAL NOUN ADJECTIVE

source of inspiration. There's Sophia, which means "one who is

_____," and Audrey, meaning "_____ strength."
ADJECTIVE ADJECTIVE

Looking for a boyish name? Try out Mackenzie, meaning "child

of the wise _____," Riley, which means "_____
NOUN ADJECTIVE

one," or Peyton, which means "warrior's _____." Cute
NOUN

names with double _____ include Charlotte, which
PLURAL NOUN

means "_____ and womanly" and Emma, which means
ADJECTIVE

"all-_____." Want a name that really sings? How about
VERB ENDING IN "ING"

Adele, meaning "_____ one," Mariah, meaning "the
ADJECTIVE

_____ of the sea," or Rihanna, which means "sweet
NOUN

_____"? If you find more than one option that floats your
NOUN

_____, you can always use one as a middle _____!
NOUN NOUN

Adult MAD LIBS

A NO-THANK-YOU NOTE

The world's greatest _shower_ game

MAD LIBS® is fun to play with friends, but you can also play it by yourself! To begin with, DO NOT look at the story on the page below. Fill in the blanks on this page with the words called for. Then, using the words you have selected, fill in the blank spaces in the story. Now you've created your own hilarious MAD LIBS® game!

PART OF THE BODY _____

NOUN _____

PERSON IN ROOM (FEMALE) _____

NUMBER _____

ADJECTIVE _____

ADJECTIVE _____

NOUN _____

NOUN _____

VERB ENDING IN "ING" _____

PLURAL NOUN _____

NOUN _____

VERB ENDING IN "ING" _____

NOUN _____

PART OF THE BODY _____

ADJECTIVE _____

NOUN _____

NOUN _____

ADJECTIVE _____

Have you gotten a baby gift that's just downright _____-ugly?

PART OF THE BODY

Here's the thank-you note you wish you could pop into the

_____ to your well-meaning but misguided friend:

NOUN

Dear _____: Wow! What an unusual, _____-of-a-

PERSON IN ROOM (FEMALE)   NUMBER

kind gift you sent us! You have such eclectic, _____ taste! It

ADJECTIVE

was too darn _____ of you to knit a baby _____ made

ADJECTIVE   NOUN

out of the scratchiest wool known to _____-kind. I'm sure our

NOUN

little one will love _____ with a piece of fabric that feels like

VERB ENDING IN "ING"

a bed of rose _____. The matching booties, hat, and burping

PLURAL NOUN

_____ will come in handy never! Also, the poster of the clown

NOUN

_____ fruit is captivating. The fact that he's also crying,

VERB ENDING IN "ING"

smoking a/an _____, and hasn't shaved his _____

NOUN   PART OF THE BODY

in weeks makes me think he might have some _____ issues. I

ADJECTIVE

can't wait not to put this up on our blank nursery _____! Plus,

NOUN

thanks for the windup stuffed _____ that plays a haunting

NOUN

version of "Mary Had a/an _____ Lamb." You shouldn't have

ADJECTIVE

gone to all the trouble . . . really.

From ADULT MAD LIBS™: Baby on Board Mad Libs • Copyright © 2013 by Price Stern Sloan, an imprint of Penguin Group (USA) Inc., 345 Hudson Street, New York, NY 10014.

MAD LIBS® is fun to play with friends, but you can also play it by yourself! To begin with, DO NOT look at the story on the page below. Fill in the blanks on this page with the words called for. Then, using the words you have selected, fill in the blank spaces in the story. Now you've created your own hilarious MAD LIBS® game!

VERB ENDING IN "ING" _____

NOUN _____

NOUN _____

PLURAL NOUN _____

ADJECTIVE _____

NOUN _____

NUMBER _____

PLURAL NOUN _____

NOUN _____

NOUN _____

VERB (PAST TENSE) _____

NOUN _____

VERB (PAST TENSE) _____

NOUN _____

NOUN _____

NUMBER _____

PART OF THE BODY _____

PART OF THE BODY _____

NUMBER _____

Adult MAD LIBS™

WORST SHOWER EVER

The world's greatest _shower_ game

Baby showers are supposed to be a day of _____ and aahing
VERB ENDING IN "ING"

over gifts and basking in the _____ of your upcoming
NOUN

arrival, right? Well, mine was a far _____ from that picture-
NOUN

perfect scenario! Basically, it sucked _____ . First off, my
PLURAL NOUN

_____ friend went balls to the _____ planning
ADJECTIVE   NOUN

everything. She sent _____ e-mails to guests with surveys
NUMBER

about which _____ to play and who was bringing what to
PLURAL NOUN

the pot- _____ luncheon. Anyone who didn't RSVP was put
NOUN

on her _____ -list. The day of the shower, the hostess acted
NOUN

like she had _____ heavily on a/an _____ pipe. First
VERB (PAST TENSE)   NOUN

she _____ at everyone to play " _____ Bingo." I
VERB (PAST TENSE)   NOUN

know, Yawnsville. Then, she had a hissy _____ when another
NOUN

friend showed up late. Her hyper _____ -year-old stuck his
NUMBER

_____ in the cake, which had a baby's head coming out of
PART OF THE BODY

a woman's _____ . Yum. Oh, and my husband showed up
PART OF THE BODY

_____ sheets to the wind after his man shower to pick me up.
NUMBER

Hey, at least _he_ had fun!

FAVORITE CRAVINGS

The world's greatest _shower_ game

MAD LIBS® is fun to play with friends, but you can also play it by yourself! To begin with, DO NOT look at the story on the page below. Fill in the blanks on this page with the words called for. Then, using the words you have selected, fill in the blank spaces in the story. Now you've created your own hilarious MAD LIBS® game!

NUMBER _____

FIRST NAME (MALE)_____

NOUN _____

VERB (PAST TENSE)_____

NOUN _____

ADJECTIVE _____

TYPE OF LIQUID _____

ADJECTIVE _____

NOUN _____

VERB_____

NOUN _____

ADJECTIVE _____

VERB_____

COLOR_____

NOUN _____

PLURAL NOUN_____

VERB (PAST TENSE)_____

Eating for _____ ? Check out this weekly roundup of food
_____NUMBER_____

cravings! Sound familiar?

Monday: At midnight, sent husband out to supermarket to buy Ben

& _____'s chocolate chip _____ dough ice cream.
___FIRST NAME (MALE)_____NOUN_____

_____ directly from container.
__VERB (PAST TENSE)__

Tuesday: In the middle of the _____ , guzzled completely
_____NOUN_____

_____ jar of pickle _____ like it was an ice-cold can
__ADJECTIVE_____TYPE OF LIQUID__

of beer. Revolting in theory, _____ in practice!
_____ADJECTIVE__

Wednesday: Mauled cupcakes with _____-flavored potato
_____NOUN___

chips crumbled on top.

Thursday: Hit the _____-thru at Burger _____ for
_____VERB_____NOUN_____

fries, dipped in mixture of _____ sauce and mustard. Don't
_____ADJECTIVE___

_____ it till you try it!
__VERB__

Friday: Added _____ olives to slice of cheese- _____ .
_____COLOR_____NOUN___

Saturday: Nachos with black _____ , cheese, and guacamole. *Olé!*
_____PLURAL NOUN__

Sunday: _____ chicken with gravy for breakfast. Hey, it's what
__VERB (PAST TENSE)__

baby wanted!

Adult MAD LIBS

BIRTH PLAN

The world's greatest _shower_ game

MAD LIBS® is fun to play with friends, but you can also play it by yourself! To begin with, DO NOT look at the story on the page below. Fill in the blanks on this page with the words called for. Then, using the words you have selected, fill in the blank spaces in the story. Now you've created your own hilarious MAD LIBS® game!

NOUN _____

NOUN _____

NOUN _____

ANIMAL_____

PLURAL NOUN_____

NUMBER _____

NOUN _____

NOUN _____

VERB_____

NOUN _____

VERB_____

NOUN _____

PART OF THE BODY _____

NOUN _____

NOUN _____

NOUN _____

ADJECTIVE _____

VERB (PAST TENSE)_____

Adult MAD LIBS™

BIRTH PLAN

The world's greatest _shower_ game

Now that you've got a/an _____ in the oven, it's time to
NOUN

plan how you're going to get him out! Do you want a birthing

_____ in the room with you? They can help to keep everyone
NOUN

calm and not freaking the _____ out. Don't worry about
NOUN

hurting your _____-in-law's feelings if you don't want her
ANIMAL

there. Seriously, who would? In early labor, many women stay at

home until their _____ are _____ minutes apart. Of
PLURAL NOUN _NUMBER_

course, call your _____ once your _____ breaks or
NOUN _NOUN_

contractions begin! Lots of hospitals let you _____ to music,
VERB

wear your own night-_____, and bring snacks. Think of
NOUN

it as a/an _____-over party, with a baby as your goody bag!
VERB

You have to decide: do you want _____ medication? Do
NOUN

you want to see the baby emerge from your _____? Will
PART OF THE BODY

your partner catch the _____ when he comes out, or cut
NOUN

the umbilical _____? Of course, things can change in a
NOUN

heart-_____, so don't be _____ if your plan gets
NOUN _ADJECTIVE_

_____ to the curb!
VERB (PAST TENSE)

MAD LIBS® is fun to play with friends, but you can also play it by yourself! To begin with, DO NOT look at the story on the page below. Fill in the blanks on this page with the words called for. Then, using the words you have selected, fill in the blank spaces in the story. Now you've created your own hilarious MAD LIBS® game!

NOUN _____

ADJECTIVE _____

NUMBER _____

ADJECTIVE _____

VERB _____

NOUN _____

PLURAL NOUN _____

ADJECTIVE _____

PLURAL NOUN _____

NOUN _____

ADJECTIVE _____

PLURAL NOUN _____

PART OF THE BODY _____

VERB ENDING IN "ING" _____

NOUN _____

NOUN _____

VERB _____

PLURAL NOUN _____

Adult MAD LIBS™
The world's greatest _shower_ game

THE JOYS OF PREGNANCY

Sure, it's truly a miracle to be growing a human _____ inside

NOUN

your body, but let's not forget about all the other _____

ADJECTIVE

changes you go through in the _____ months leading up

NUMBER

to the _____ event! One of the most common pregnancy

ADJECTIVE

symptoms is the urge to _____ up. Without warning, that

VERB

pepperoni _____ you used to drool over becomes your worst

NOUN

enemy, and saltine _____ become your best friend. Then

PLURAL NOUN

there are the _____ hormones flooding your system. Hello,

ADJECTIVE

red _____ on your face and rampant _____ swings!

PLURAL NOUN   NOUN

It's like having your " _____ time of the month" every day.

ADJECTIVE

Then, as you get bigger, your stomach _____ get squished.

PLURAL NOUN

The result? A case of _____-burn so bad you wonder

PART OF THE BODY

if there's a tiny fire-_____ dragon living in your throat.

VERB ENDING IN "ING"

Another change is how much you use the bath-_____. It's

NOUN

like your bladder shrinks to the size of a/an _____. A mere

NOUN

laugh, sneeze, or _____ can make you rethink wearing adult

VERB

_____. You won't, but you'll wish you were!

PLURAL NOUN

MAD LIBS® is fun to play with friends, but you can also play it by yourself! To begin with, DO NOT look at the story on the page below. Fill in the blanks on this page with the words called for. Then, using the words you have selected, fill in the blank spaces in the story. Now you've created your own hilarious MAD LIBS® game!

VERB ENDING IN "ING" _____

NOUN _____

ADJECTIVE _____

NOUN _____

NUMBER _____

PLURAL NOUN _____

NOUN _____

PART OF THE BODY (PLURAL) _____

VERB _____

LETTER OF THE ALPHABET _____

PLURAL NOUN _____

VERB _____

PLURAL NOUN _____

PLURAL NOUN _____

ADJECTIVE _____

NOUN _____

PLURAL NOUN _____

PART OF THE BODY _____

Before you know it, your baby is going to be _____ all over

VERB ENDING IN "ING"

the house and picking up every loose _____ on the floor

NOUN

for a taste test! Check out our guide to keeping your munchkin

safe and _____ . To avoid scorching water coming out of

ADJECTIVE

the faucet, set your _____ heater to _____ degrees.

NOUN NUMBER

Keep electrical _____ out of reach, and cover _____

PLURAL NOUN NOUN

sockets to prevent baby from jolting his little _____ .

PART OF THE BODY (PLURAL)

When it comes to snacks, stay clear of hard-to- _____

VERB

foods like grapes and popcorn. If your baby chokes, it's a good

idea to know how to do infant CP- _____ ! Got lots

LETTER OF THE ALPHABET

of dangling curtain _____ around? Tie 'em up so baby

PLURAL NOUN

doesn't _____ them around his neck! In the crib, get rid of

VERB

blankets and stuffed _____ to avoid suffocation. Use drawer

PLURAL NOUN

_____ on cabinets so baby can't get into the bottle of Mr.

PLURAL NOUN

_____ cleaner. Install carbon _____ detectors with

ADJECTIVE NOUN

fresh _____ inside. It's a lot of work, but worth the peace of

PLURAL NOUN

_____ !

PART OF THE BODY

Adult MAD LIBS — OLD WIVES' TALES

The world's greatest _shower_ game

MAD LIBS® is fun to play with friends, but you can also play it by yourself! To begin with, DO NOT look at the story on the page below. Fill in the blanks on this page with the words called for. Then, using the words you have selected, fill in the blank spaces in the story. Now you've created your own hilarious MAD LIBS® game!

PLURAL NOUN _____

PLURAL NOUN _____

ADJECTIVE _____

PART OF THE BODY _____

PLURAL NOUN _____

NOUN _____

ADJECTIVE _____

PLURAL NOUN _____

VERB ENDING IN "ING" _____

NUMBER _____

ADJECTIVE _____

NOUN _____

NOUN _____

ADJECTIVE _____

NOUN _____

VERB ENDING IN "ING" _____

ADJECTIVE _____

NOUN _____

Are you full-term and eager for your _____ to start?

PLURAL NOUN

Heed the wisdom from these old _____' tales to kick

PLURAL NOUN

labor into _____ gear! One trick is to stimulate the

ADJECTIVE

_____, which can then stimulate the uterus. Get some red

PART OF THE BODY

curry in a hurry! Try eating spicy _____, or swallowing a

PLURAL NOUN

spoonful of _____ oil. If you can handle being stuck with

NOUN

super-_____ needles, acupuncture can open up energy

ADJECTIVE

_____ in your body. Some say _____ pineapple can

PLURAL NOUN VERB ENDING IN "ING"

soften the cervix—but you'd need to eat _____ servings for

NUMBER

any possible effect. Um, diarrhea, anyone? Another tactic is to go

on _____ walks around your _____-hood to get

ADJECTIVE NOUN

baby moving down the birth _____. The most fun idea?

NOUN

Getting down and _____ with your hubby! The release of

ADJECTIVE

oxytocin, the "_____ hormone," precedes contractions.

NOUN

And hey, even if _____ the deed doesn't work, at least you

VERB ENDING IN "ING"

had a/an _____ time before baby puts a damper on your

ADJECTIVE

_____ life!

NOUN

MAD LIBS® is fun to play with friends, but you can also play it by yourself! To begin with, DO NOT look at the story on the page below. Fill in the blanks on this page with the words called for. Then, using the words you have selected, fill in the blank spaces in the story. Now you've created your own hilarious MAD LIBS® game!

VERB ENDING IN "ING" _____

PLURAL NOUN _____

NOUN _____

VERB _____

NOUN _____

PART OF THE BODY _____

ADJECTIVE _____

VERB ENDING IN "ING" _____

PLURAL NOUN _____

ADJECTIVE _____

PART OF THE BODY _____

VERB ENDING IN "ING" _____

NUMBER _____

VERB ENDING IN "ING" _____

PLURAL NOUN _____

NOUN _____

PLURAL NOUN _____

NOUN _____

Adult MAD LIBS™ HOME BIRTH

The world's greatest _shower_ game

Planning on _____ out your bundle of _____ in the
 VERB ENDING IN "ING"   PLURAL NOUN

comfort of your own _____? Get prepared with the following
 NOUN

to- _____ list! First, you'll need a certified mid- _____
 VERB   NOUN

for delivery. In case of an emergency, pick one who has a solid

_____ -up plan for care. Try music and _____ lighting
 PART OF THE BODY   ADJECTIVE

to set the mood—like a romantic night in, except with lots more

_____! To get ready, you'll want to protect your bed from
 VERB ENDING IN "ING"

bodily _____ with a plastic sheet. Or you could grab a bunch
 PLURAL NOUN

of _____ towels and use them to absorb whatever flies out of
 ADJECTIVE

your _____! You might consider renting a/an _____
 PART OF THE BODY   VERB ENDING IN "ING"

tub. It's the one type of bath in which it's okay to go number

_____. Many women even give birth underwater. You can
 NUMBER

brag that your baby started _____ at a really young age. Get
 VERB ENDING IN "ING"

two clamps and a pair of sterile _____ for when it's time to cut
 PLURAL NOUN

the umbilical cord. Don't forget to buy a squirt _____ to rinse
 NOUN

with postpartum. Your nether _____ will be sore and may
 PLURAL NOUN

sting like a mother- _____!
 NOUN

Adult MAD LIBS™

WELCOME TO MOMMYHOOD

The world's greatest _shower_ game

MAD LIBS® is fun to play with friends, but you can also play it by yourself! To begin with, DO NOT look at the story on the page below. Fill in the blanks on this page with the words called for. Then, using the words you have selected, fill in the blank spaces in the story. Now you've created your own hilarious MAD LIBS® game!

VERB (PAST TENSE) _____

PART OF THE BODY _____

VERB _____

NUMBER _____

VERB _____

NOUN _____

ADJECTIVE _____

VERB _____

ADJECTIVE _____

VERB _____

NOUN _____

NOUN _____

VERB _____

NOUN _____

PART OF THE BODY _____

ADJECTIVE _____

VERB ENDING IN "ING" _____

WELCOME TO MOMMYHOOD

The world's greatest _shower_ game

After giving birth, you'll probably feel like you just _____ a
VERB (PAST TENSE)

marathon! A tip? Take advantage of any shut- _____ you can
PART OF THE BODY

snag in the hospital. New parenthood basically means you won't get

to _____ for the next few months, since newborns need to be
VERB

fed every two to _____ hours. The days will _____
NUMBER VERB

together as you become _____ -deprived, which can drive
NOUN

you a bit _____ . Make sure you _____ down
ADJECTIVE VERB

when your baby is conked out. Feel like a prisoner? Get some

_____ air with a walk around the block. Exercise will
ADJECTIVE

help _____ the jiggle in your wiggle! Enlist your partner,
VERB

mom, or a/an _____ -sitter for help. Sneak away for a little
NOUN

" _____ " time to re- _____ your batteries, even
NOUN VERB

if it's just to hide in the bathroom to read a trashy _____ .
NOUN

Getting it on with your sweetie might be the last thing on your

_____ . It's normal to have a long _____ spell. Stay
PART OF THE BODY ADJECTIVE

close with lots of _____ instead!
VERB ENDING IN "ING"

Adult MAD LIBS™ LABOR MIX

The world's greatest *shower* game

MAD LIBS® is fun to play with friends, but you can also play it by yourself! To begin with, DO NOT look at the story on the page below. Fill in the blanks on this page with the words called for. Then, using the words you have selected, fill in the blank spaces in the story. Now you've created your own hilarious MAD LIBS® game!

VERB ENDING IN "ING" _____

VERB _____

NOUN _____

ADJECTIVE _____

ADJECTIVE _____

COLOR _____

NOUN _____

FIRST NAME (MALE) _____

NOUN _____

COLOR _____

NOUN _____

PLURAL NOUN _____

VERB _____

FIRST NAME (FEMALE) _____

VERB ENDING IN "ING" _____

FIRST NAME (FEMALE) _____

Adult MAD LIBS™ LABOR MIX

The world's greatest _shower_ game

Wish you had a motivating sound track to keep you energized during

labor? Cue up this mix of classic songs for when you're in the throes

of fist- _____ contractions!
        VERB ENDING IN "ING"

1. " _____ It," by Salt-N- _____ —This ladies' rap
        VERB   NOUN

anthem will get you to "push it real _____ "!
                                      ADJECTIVE

2. "Comfortably _____ ," by _____ Floyd—Perfect
                 ADJECTIVE   COLOR

for when the epidural kicks in.

3. " _____ -ville," by _____ Buffett—Focus on
        NOUN   FIRST NAME (MALE)

celebrating with a margarita!

4. "Get This _____ Started," by _____ —Because
              NOUN   COLOR

labor is a nonstop party!

5. "Sweet _____ o' Mine," by _____ N' Roses—
           NOUN   PLURAL NOUN

Great to scream along to!

6. " _____ Baby," by _____ Joplin—Get ready to
        VERB   FIRST NAME (FEMALE)

hear your baby cry for the first time!

7. "I'm _____ Out," by _____ Ross—The ultimate
         VERB ENDING IN "ING"   FIRST NAME (FEMALE)

finale.

Adult MAD LIBS

SAFETY RECALLS

The world's greatest *shower* game

MAD LIBS® is fun to play with friends, but you can also play it by yourself! To begin with, DO NOT look at the story on the page below. Fill in the blanks on this page with the words called for. Then, using the words you have selected, fill in the blank spaces in the story. Now you've created your own hilarious MAD LIBS® game!

NOUN _____

NUMBER _____

VERB_____

NOUN _____

VERB_____

NUMBER _____

NOUN _____

ADJECTIVE _____

NOUN _____

NOUN _____

NOUN _____

NOUN _____

NUMBER _____

ADJECTIVE _____

PLURAL NOUN_____

PLURAL NOUN_____

VERB_____

VERB_____

Adult MAD LIBS

SAFETY RECALLS

The world's greatest _shower_ game

Oh my _____ , I'm so excited you're pregnant! Can I tell you

NOUN

something, though? As a mother of _____ , I'm kind of a/

NUMBER

an _____ -it-all when it comes to which products to avoid.

VERB

You've got to stay up-to- _____ on this stuff, unless you want

NOUN

to accidentally _____ your baby, ha-ha! Seriously though,

VERB

I spend _____ hours a day scouring the Internet for safety

NUMBER

recalls. There's this one crib where if the _____ jumps too

NOUN

hard, the sides collapse! Can you imagine? And then I just read about

this "all- _____ " baby food that has traces of _____

ADJECTIVE   NOUN

in it. If you're like me, you'll make your own _____ after

NOUN

you do some research. Also, be really careful about _____

NOUN

seats. So many of them are _____ traps! I just use my own

NOUN

_____ legs to take my kids everywhere. Diapers are also a/an

NUMBER

_____ no-no. They're filled with all kinds of _____ . I

ADJECTIVE   PLURAL NOUN

relied on reading my baby's facial _____ to determine when he

PLURAL NOUN

needed to go. Then, I'd just _____ him over the toilet! See? As

VERB

long as you take precautions, there's nothing to _____ about!

VERB

Adult MAD LIBS™

DECODING THE DIAPER

The world's greatest *shower* game

MAD LIBS® is fun to play with friends, but you can also play it by yourself! To begin with, DO NOT look at the story on the page below. Fill in the blanks on this page with the words called for. Then, using the words you have selected, fill in the blank spaces in the story. Now you've created your own hilarious MAD LIBS® game!

ADJECTIVE _____

VERB ENDING IN "ING" _____

ADJECTIVE _____

PLURAL NOUN _____

ADJECTIVE _____

VERB ENDING IN "ING" _____

VERB ENDING IN "ING" _____

NOUN _____

NOUN _____

NOUN _____

VERB _____

PLURAL NOUN _____

ADJECTIVE _____

PLURAL NOUN _____

LETTER OF THE ALPHABET _____

What's that black, _____ stuff inside baby's first diaper?
ADJECTIVE

And why is it _____ a different color every few days? Get
VERB ENDING IN "ING"

the scoop on your darling's poops! Babies are born with meconium

inside of them. It's dark and quite _____, like motor oil.
ADJECTIVE

Vroom, vroom! When baby is two to four _____ old, his
PLURAL NOUN

poop will get lighter and less _____. This means that he's
ADJECTIVE

_____ food correctly, so yay! If you're breast-_____,
VERB ENDING IN "ING"   VERB ENDING IN "ING"

the diaper fairies will leave you with a more yellow poop. It will

remind you of Dijon _____ and cottage _____,
NOUN   NOUN

two things that will now gross you out forever! Are you giving

baby formula? Then his "gifts" will be more tannish brown, and

they'll have a consistency like peanut _____. Hey, you can
NOUN

_____ that off your want-to-eat list, too! If his poop looks
VERB

like a bunch of _____, baby could be backed up. Also, if the
PLURAL NOUN

diaper looks like a/an _____ river, then baby might have the
ADJECTIVE

runs. Babies go through a hundred _____ in the first week.
PLURAL NOUN

By the end of it you'll have a Ph-_____ in poopology!
LETTER OF THE ALPHABET

MAD LIBS® is fun to play with friends, but you can also play it by yourself! To begin with, DO NOT look at the story on the page below. Fill in the blanks on this page with the words called for. Then, using the words you have selected, fill in the blank spaces in the story. Now you've created your own hilarious MAD LIBS® game!

NOUN _____

PART OF THE BODY _____

NOUN _____

VERB ENDING IN "ING" _____

NOUN _____

PLURAL NOUN _____

EXCLAMATION _____

VERB ENDING IN "ING" _____

NOUN _____

NOUN _____

TYPE OF LIQUID _____

NOUN _____

NUMBER _____

PLURAL NOUN _____

VERB _____

NOUN _____

PART OF THE BODY (PLURAL) _____

ADJECTIVE _____

Adult MAD LIBS™
THE DAY I FOUND OUT I WAS PREGNANT

The world's greatest _shower_ game

Realizing you have a/an _____ inside of your _____

NOUN · PART OF THE BODY

is a moment you never forget! What made you suspect you might

be pregnant? Did you miss your monthly _____ ? Or

NOUN

maybe you just had a/an _____ suspicion because, oops,

VERB ENDING IN "ING"

the _____ broke! Probably the first thing you did was run

NOUN

to the drugstore to buy a slew of pregnancy _____ . There's

PLURAL NOUN

the kind that just says " _____ !"/"No" and the kind with

EXCLAMATION

the plus/minus sign. Isn't _____ on that stick the most

VERB ENDING IN "ING"

nerve-racking thing ever? Your mind races with a million thoughts:

Am I ready to be a/an _____ ? What will my _____

NOUN · NOUN

think? How can a drop of _____ tell me so much?! And

TYPE OF LIQUID

then, holy _____ ! The test is positive. So of course you do

NOUN

_____ more just to make sure! Did you cry _____ of

NUMBER · PLURAL NOUN

joy? Perhaps you felt a rush of adrenaline _____ through your

VERB

veins. You might've wondered how to tell your other _____ .

NOUN

Hopefully, the result was met with open _____ and not

PART OF THE BODY (PLURAL)

_____ shock!

ADJECTIVE

Adult MAD LIBS

THE ULTIMATE DIAPER BAG

The world's greatest _shower_ game

MAD LIBS® is fun to play with friends, but you can also play it by yourself! To begin with, DO NOT look at the story on the page below. Fill in the blanks on this page with the words called for. Then, using the words you have selected, fill in the blank spaces in the story. Now you've created your own hilarious MAD LIBS® game!

PLURAL NOUN _____

NOUN _____

PLURAL NOUN _____

NUMBER _____

ADJECTIVE _____

NOUN _____

VERB ENDING IN "ING" _____

PART OF THE BODY (PLURAL) _____

NOUN _____

NOUN _____

VERB ENDING IN "ING" _____

VERB _____

PLURAL NOUN _____

PLURAL NOUN _____

VERB _____

PLURAL NOUN _____

VERB ENDING IN "ING" _____

PLURAL NOUN _____

Packing a diaper bag is one of those tasks that stresses new

_____ out. It should be simple, so why does it feel so
<u>PLURAL NOUN</u>

complicated? Here, we'll break out a/an _____ -proof strategy
<u>NOUN</u>

for making sure you're stocked with all the right stuff! Obviously,

you need fresh _____ . Include about _____ for
<u>PLURAL NOUN</u>   <u>NUMBER</u>

every hour you'll be away. Stick a wad of _____ wipes in a
<u>ADJECTIVE</u>

plastic _____ . They'll work double duty for _____
<u>NOUN</u>   <u>VERB ENDING IN "ING"</u>

both your baby's tush and also your _____ if they get caught
<u>PART OF THE BODY (PLURAL)</u>

in the line of fire! Add a tube of _____ cream in case baby's
<u>NOUN</u>

_____ is irritated. A/An _____ pad, a bottle of
<u>NOUN</u>   <u>VERB ENDING IN "ING"</u>

milk or formula, and a blanket are essential, too. If baby has a/an

_____ -out and you-know-what splatters everywhere, a
<u>VERB</u>

change of _____ will save the day! Or at least the hour.
<u>PLURAL NOUN</u>

A few burp _____ are good to have in case baby has a/an
<u>PLURAL NOUN</u>

_____ -up session. Are you whipping out your _____
<u>VERB</u>   <u>PLURAL NOUN</u>

in public for feedings? You may want a/an _____ cover to
<u>VERB ENDING IN "ING"</u>

keep creepy _____ from staring at you!
<u>PLURAL NOUN</u>

MAD LIBS® is fun to play with friends, but you can also play it by yourself! To begin with, DO NOT look at the story on the page below. Fill in the blanks on this page with the words called for. Then, using the words you have selected, fill in the blank spaces in the story. Now you've created your own hilarious MAD LIBS® game!

ADJECTIVE _____

NOUN _____

ADJECTIVE _____

VERB_____

NOUN _____

ANIMAL _____

PART OF THE BODY _____

NOUN _____

ADJECTIVE _____

NOUN _____

VERB ENDING IN "ING" _____

NOUN _____

PART OF THE BODY _____

ADJECTIVE _____

NOUN _____

NOUN _____

Adult MAD LIBS™

BABY SHOWER GAMES

The world's greatest _shower_ game

They're kind of hokey, but the tried-and- _____ tradition of

ADJECTIVE

baby shower games is a good _____ -breaker if your guests

NOUN

don't all know one another. Here are some versions that even your

most _____ -puss pal will get a/an _____ out of. Or

ADJECTIVE · VERB

at least she'll enjoy making fun of them!

- "Stick the _____ in Baby's Mouth"—This game works just

NOUN

  like "Pin the Tail on the _____," except the goal is to tape

ANIMAL

  a pacifier drawing onto a picture of a baby's _____. For a

PART OF THE BODY

  racier option, you can easily change this game to "Stick the Sperm

  on the Ovulating _____"!

NOUN

- "Pass the _____ Diaper"—Remember the game "Hot

ADJECTIVE

  _____"? Same rules, except a group of women sit in a

NOUN

  circle _____ around a diaper filled with warm brown

VERB ENDING IN "ING"

  _____ sauce. Yum!

NOUN

- "Guess Mom's _____ Size"—Guesstimate how

PART OF THE BODY

  _____ the _____ -to-be's tummy is by cutting a

ADJECTIVE · NOUN

  piece of _____ the guests think will fit around her belly.

NOUN

Adult
MAD LIBS

PAIN MANAGEMENT SEGMENT

The world's greatest _shower_ game

MAD LIBS® is fun to play with friends, but you can also play it by yourself! To begin with, DO NOT look at the story on the page below. Fill in the blanks on this page with the words called for. Then, using the words you have selected, fill in the blank spaces in the story. Now you've created your own hilarious MAD LIBS® game!

FIRST NAME (MALE) _____

SAME FIRST NAME (MALE) _____

NOUN _____

PART OF THE BODY _____

VERB ENDING IN "ING" _____

PART OF THE BODY _____

ADJECTIVE _____

VERB ENDING IN "ING" _____

NOUN _____

VERB _____

NOUN _____

ADJECTIVE _____

PLURAL NOUN _____

NOUN _____

PART OF THE BODY _____

NUMBER _____

ADJECTIVE _____

VERB ENDING IN "ING" _____

Hi, I'm Dr. _____ , star of TV's hit talk show _Dr._
_{FIRST NAME (MALE)}

_____ ! Today's topic is all about pain management during
_{SAME FIRST NAME (MALE)}

labor. First, I want to mention some _____ -free methods
_{NOUN}

to try. Have you heard the expression " _____ over matter"?
_{PART OF THE BODY}

Relaxing your brain will keep your body from _____ up
_{VERB ENDING IN "ING"}

during contractions. _____ in hand with relaxing is to
_{PART OF THE BODY}

focus on _____ breathing. Low, guttural _____
_{ADJECTIVE} _{VERB ENDING IN "ING"}

can help you get through a rough moment. Don't worry about

sounding like a wounded _____ about to keel over and
_{NOUN}

_____ ! Rolling on a birthing _____ , taking a/an
_{VERB} _{NOUN}

_____ bath, and getting massaged are good options, too.
_{ADJECTIVE}

Now, how about those powerful _____ ? The most common
_{PLURAL NOUN}

_____ -killer is the epidural. All it takes is a teeny hole in the
_{NOUN}

_____ to inject the medicine! It takes ten to _____
_{PART OF THE BODY} _{NUMBER}

minutes to work. Tranquilizers lessen anxiety, but they may leave you

feeling _____ around the edges, like you're _____
_{ADJECTIVE} _{VERB ENDING IN "ING"}

high in the sky!

Adult MAD LIBS

The world's greatest _shower_ game

BREAST-FEEDING 101

MAD LIBS® is fun to play with friends, but you can also play it by yourself! To begin with, DO NOT look at the story on the page below. Fill in the blanks on this page with the words called for. Then, using the words you have selected, fill in the blank spaces in the story. Now you've created your own hilarious MAD LIBS® game!

PART OF THE BODY (PLURAL) _____

VERB ENDING IN "ING" _____

NOUN _____

NOUN _____

NOUN _____

PLURAL NOUN _____

PLURAL NOUN _____

VERB ENDING IN "ING" _____

NOUN _____

ADJECTIVE _____

PART OF THE BODY _____

VERB ENDING IN "ING" _____

VERB _____

NOUN _____

NUMBER _____

PLURAL NOUN _____

VERB ENDING IN "ING" _____

NOUN _____

Planning on nourishing your baby with your giant _____?

PART OF THE BODY (PLURAL)

Here are some tips on how to tackle breast- _____ , even

VERB ENDING IN "ING"

when they feel as if they've been run over by a/an _____!

NOUN

Try to begin as soon as your _____ is born. It's a great way

NOUN

to bond, plus it's a/an _____ burner! Make sure you have

NOUN

plenty of _____ to support your arms, or baby will feel like

PLURAL NOUN

a ton of _____ . Avoid _____ forward, and bring

PLURAL NOUN · VERB ENDING IN "ING"

baby to your _____ instead. For a/an _____ latch,

NOUN · ADJECTIVE

her _____ should fully enclose the whole nipple region. If she

PART OF THE BODY

establishes a sucking-and- _____ rhythm, then she's gotten

VERB ENDING IN "ING"

into the groove! Give baby time to _____ to make room for

VERB

more of your liquid _____ . When boob #1 gets soft, it's

NOUN

time for baby to drain boob # _____ . Does one side feel as

NUMBER

if it's full of hard _____ ? Try _____ some milk out

PLURAL NOUN · VERB ENDING IN "ING"

to relieve the pressure. If your nipples feel as if they've been attacked

by a/an _____ -thirsty vampire, rub some lanolin cream on

NOUN

them. In a few weeks, they'll toughen up!

MAD LIBS® is fun to play with friends, but you can also play it by yourself! To begin with, DO NOT look at the story on the page below. Fill in the blanks on this page with the words called for. Then, using the words you have selected, fill in the blank spaces in the story. Now you've created your own hilarious MAD LIBS® game!

ADJECTIVE _____

VERB _____

ADJECTIVE _____

A PLACE _____

NOUN _____

VERB ENDING IN "ING" _____

VERB _____

NOUN _____

PLURAL NOUN _____

NUMBER _____

NOUN _____

VERB _____

COLOR _____

NOUN _____

PART OF THE BODY _____

VERB ENDING IN "ING" _____

NOUN _____

PLURAL NOUN _____

Adult MAD LIBS™ POSTPARTUM PLEASURES

The world's greatest _shower_ game

When you get so big that you feel like a double-_____ trailer,
ADJECTIVE

think about all the things you'll be able to eat and _____
VERB

once your baby is born! Since _____ foods like sushi
ADJECTIVE

are a preggo no-no, imagine a feast of (the) _____ rolls
A PLACE

and _____ tartare. Oooh, and a plate of fresh oysters
NOUN

_____ down your throat! Take that, listeria! Your mouth
VERB ENDING IN "ING"

might _____ at the thought of a toasted bagel with cream
VERB

cheese and smoked _____. Soon, it will be yours to savor!
NOUN

Now onto the sweet nectar of the _____—wine! Maybe
PLURAL NOUN

you've had a sip or _____ during pregnancy, but now you
NUMBER

can enjoy it _____-free. Just pump and _____
NOUN VERB

if you're breast-feeding! How awesome will it be to go out and

order a _____ Goose on the rocks? Or drink some spiked
COLOR

_____ cider with your honey by the fire? Speaking
NOUN

of romance, postbaby you won't have that huge _____ to
PART OF THE BODY

get in the way during love-_____. Just make sure to use
VERB ENDING IN "ING"

_____ control—unless you want a pair of Irish _____!
NOUN PLURAL NOUN

Adult MAD LIBS™

YOUR BABY IS SO, UM, CUTE

The world's greatest _shower_ game

MAD LIBS® is fun to play with friends, but you can also play it by yourself! To begin with, DO NOT look at the story on the page below. Fill in the blanks on this page with the words called for. Then, using the words you have selected, fill in the blank spaces in the story. Now you've created your own hilarious MAD LIBS® game!

VERB _____

ADJECTIVE _____

VERB ENDING IN "ING" _____

FIRST NAME (MALE)_____

VERB _____

NOUN _____

NOUN _____

ADJECTIVE _____

PART OF THE BODY _____

VERB (PAST TENSE)_____

PART OF THE BODY _____

NOUN _____

VERB _____

NOUN _____

Here's what to say when your friend has a baby who has looks he'll

_____ into: Awww, look at your precious, _____
    VERB   ADJECTIVE

peanut! Why no, I didn't notice that he has a/an _____ eye.
                                            VERB ENDING IN "ING"

I'm sure that will correct itself in no time. Yeah, I guess you could

say he got _____'s nose. All the better to _____
          FIRST NAME (MALE)   VERB

with, right? Well, will you look at that! What an interesting shape

for a birth-_____. It looks like a little teddy _____
             NOUN   NOUN

tattoo on his forehead! Wait, why are you crying? Your baby is flat-

out _____, and don't let anyone tell you differently! So what
          ADJECTIVE

if he has a sixth _____. Who's going to notice? Besides,
                   PART OF THE BODY

with modern medicine, he could get it _____ off eventually.
                                    VERB (PAST TENSE)

There, feel better? Your baby is an angel! An angel who, whoa, has a

very unique hair pattern on his _____. Lucky you, he has a
                                    PART OF THE BODY

protective layer of _____ to keep him warm! Don't worry, of
                      NOUN

course he'll shed it soon. No, his ears do not _____ out! Now
                                      VERB

you're just being crazy. And there's nothing wrong with his head being

a little _____-shaped. He can always wear a helmet to cover it!
          NOUN

Enjoy more ADULT MAD LIBS™ from

PSS!
PRICE STERN SLOAN

Countdown to Midnight Mad Libs

Log On to Mad Libs

My Bleeping Family Mad Libs

Party Girl Mad Libs

Pigskin Party Mad Libs